Scorpions

Amazing Animal Books
For Young Readers

John Davidson
Mendon Cottage Books

JD-Biz Publishing

Download Free Books!

http://MendonCottageBooks.com

All Rights Reserved.

No part of this publication may be reproduced in any form or by any means, including scanning, photocopying, or otherwise without prior written permission from JD-Biz Corp Copyright © 2015. All Images Licensed by Fotolia and 123RF.

[Read More Amazing Animal Books](#)

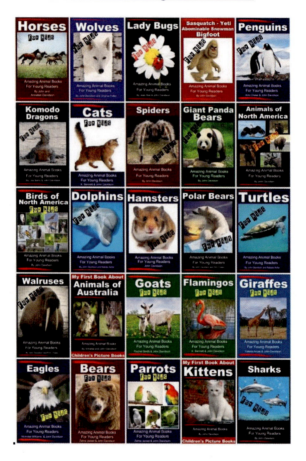

Purchase at Amazon.com

. **Download Free Books!**

http://MendonCottageBooks.com

Table of Contents

1. Classification of the scorpion 4
2. Descriptions 5
3. The behavior of the scorpions, ... 6
4. Habitats of the scorpions 7
5. Biology of the animal 10
    Scorpion Body Parts 10
    Parts of the body 10
6. Food habits of the scorpions 17
7. Some deadly species of scorpions 19
8. Scorpions and the human 25
9. Myths and stories about scorpions 27
    Publisher 36

1. Classification of the scorpion

- Kingdom   –Animalia
- Phylum   -Athropoda
- Subphylum - Chelicerata
- Class   - Aracnid
- Subclass   –Dromopoda
- Order   –Scorpiones
- Super families- Buthoidea,Chaerilodea,Choctoidea and Ivroidea

2. Descriptions

Do not be afraid and feel sick by seeing these creatures, as they are also a part of the Earth. They are predator and they are classified as anthropoids. They are included in the class Arachnida and they are in the order Scorpionses.

They have 8 legs and their have a pair of dangerous looking claws and narrow partitioned tail. Those features create the unique picture of this awesome creature. The tail is consisted with a special organ that is used to inject venom to its pray. The venom comes from 2 glands and it is very useful in hunting as well as self defence. They do not have a skeleton inside the body but they have a shell or exoskeleton out side of the body. That structure is made of a substance called chitin. Their size is between 9MM-20CM..But there are larger species in certain parts of the world.

These wonderful creatures cover entire globe except Antarctica. It can live in various habitats, but unfortunately it can not be found in high latitudes of Tundra. The scientists have recorded more than 13 families so far and 1,752 sub species. It is said that those scorpions have venom, which is capable of killing people, but it is not a correct assumption. Only 20 killer species are found from the entire number of species. That is a good news fro the nature lovers. They can have the pleasure of the nature, without fearing deadly scorpions. The scorpions have along history in the evolution. As a whole they are considered as venomous and deadly living entities.

3. The behavior of the scorpions,

The scorpions are not ready or eager to fight. They have natural tendency for escaping than facing the danger. As a whole all the scorpions are venomous in various extents. The most poisonous one is the bark scorpion, which lives in New Mexico, Arizona and some parts of California. It is so dangerous that the patient should be treated as soon as possible.

The venom of the bark scorpion is allergic to the young children and the elders. The people are lucky there was not any death related to scorpion sting since 1960 in Arizona.

4. Habitats of the scorpions

Some common habitats

A highly venomous Arabian scorpion, Apistobuthus pterygocerus, leaving its tracks on a sand dune in the Empty Quarter Desert.

A desert scorpion in its habitat

They can be seen in almost all continents of the world except Antarctica. They do not live in that ice continent. The countries such as England, New zeal land and some island of the Oceania do not have scorpions in natural habitat. They can be found in zoological gardens and exhibitions. Some animal traders and collectors have introduced scorpions in to those countries in the secret manner.

There are large numbers of species in the subtropical areas of the Northern Hemisphere. They can be found in the latitudes 23 N and 38 N. Beyond this latitude there are only limited number of species. There are some countries, which do not have natural population of scorpions. Most of the deadly scorpion species were introduced to the Europe from African continent by ancient sailors. There are 5 colonies of scorpions in Sheemess on the isle of Sheppey, which belonged to the UK. They have been there since 1860. It is believed that they have been smuggled among the fruits from the Africa. They are not dangerous to the people.

Today scorpions are found in all terrestrial habitats and they live in high mountains, caves and intertidal zones. They can not live in boreal ecosystems, so they are not established in tundra and taiga systems as well as snow capped mountainous areas.

They live in micro habitats and they can be divided in to some classes according to their place of living. There are three types of scorpions according to the habitat, which they prefer to live.

1. Ground dwelling/Tree living-
2. Rock living-
3. Sand living-

Temperature they prefer.

These scorpions prefer to reside in the tropical and subtropical climates. These creatures love to dwell in the areas, where the temperatures range from 20 to 37 °C (68 to 99 °F), but they can survive in temperatures ranging from well below freezing to desert heat.

There are some species of scorpions, which have been altered to face the environment that they have to live. The members of the genus *Scorpiops,* which are in the high Asian mountains, the *Bouthriurid* scorpions of Patagonia and the small scorpions of *Euscorpius* in central Europe, can survive in very low temperatures. They can bear a low temperature such as −25 °C (−13 °F) in the winter season.

5. Biology of the animal

Life span

It is not easy to find actual life span of most of the species. The average is between 4-25 years. The maximum life span is estimated in the species (*Hadrurus arizonensis*). They enjoy an average life span of 25-30 years in their natural habitats.

Appearance of the scorpion

Scorpion Body Parts

The appearance of the scorpion is not a very attractive but it is very interesting to learn about this age old companion of the mankind. It has many altered parts in his outer appearance as well as the inner constructions in order too face the hardships of the environment.

Parts of the body

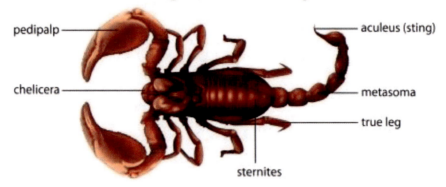

Chelicerae

Cephalothorax

Masosomal tergites

Telson

Pedipalp

Prosoma

Optithasoma

Metasomal Segments

The body is divided into three segments and these are three main parts of the body.

- The crosoma or cephalothorax- head section
- The mesosoma – abdomen section
- The metasoma - tail section

The prosoma

This section is consisted of eyes, mouth and the pair of claws, which are named as pedipalps. To add more versatility to the life, they have pincers at the end they are called as chelae. Pediplaps are not legs. They are used to grab and holding motions of the animal. They are extremely helpful in the process of feeding.

The mesosoma

This part is consisted with 4 pairs of legs. Those legs help it a lot to walk as well as to climb on any type of surface. This segment is very important, as it contains the organs for the reproduction and the respiration of the scorpion.

The metasoma

This part is the most useful and the unique part to the scorpion. The tail is made up of 5 segments and it ends at the Telson. There are 2 venom glands at Telson. The stringer or the venom injecting tool is also located in the Telson.

Scorpion Anatomy

- The male scorpions are larger than the female scorpions and they are in different colors they can be found in tan brown or florescent form of green. The color helps them to get away from the danger from the outside. And to lie and catch the pray.
- The scorpions have lot of eyes but hey have a very bad vision. They have 6-12 eyes. The scorpions are very sensitive to light; the scorpions like to get away from the sources of light. They prefer to live in dark and gloomy places.
- The body is covered with tiny and very light hairs.
- Their sense of smell is very good. So they can identify food, danger and opposite sex. The scorpions are dependent on their sense of smell than the vision.
- They can move very fast so that it is not easy to catch them. They lie in the ground and they run very fat to their pray,
- They have 8 legs and those are thicker than the legs of spiders.

- The scorpions have to pass through several stages of molting. They shed their exoskeleton, when they pass through molting stages. Exoskeleton is similar to a shell of and it has the purpose of protecting internal organs and giving support to the muscles of the body.
- They suck the liquids of the pray. They have claw like protrusions in the mouth.
- Their digestive system is not developed, so they can not consume solid food items.
- There are enzymes in the venom and it turns the pray in to liquid and the scorpion consumes the liquid.
- The venom they inject to the pray also carries some enzymes, and those enzymes digest the pray. Later the scorpion consumes half digested flesh of the victim.
- The tail is consisted with 5 segments, it is very flexible. At the end of the tail you can find the tip and there is the stinger.
- The stringer is a tough object, which can penetrate the skin of the pray and inject the venom into the body of the victim.
- They have a very slow and body metabolism, so they need only limited amount of energy to live. When there is not food they can survive a longer time and they store lot of food, when they have enough.
- They have to pass several molting stages until age 6.then they become matured. The process is very slow, when we compare with other arachnids.

- The venom is unique to each and every species, so it is very difficult for the researches to find an anti venom for them.

Reproduction

Reproduction is very important process to maintain the population of the species, among the scorpions sexual reproduction and another form of a sexual production can be found. Most of the species of the scorpions give birth to off springs by sexual reproduction. The male and female animals can attract to each other by vibrations and pheromones. They perform a special dance in the process of attraction. The fertile eggs turn into a living embryo and later turn in to a new life. In some species the unfertile eggs turn in to living embryos and later to new offspring. Those species make their new offspring without sexual mating or a relationship. This process is known as parthenogenesis. After the sexual mating is completed the male animals have to y move away from the place, as their female partners prefer to have their males as food.

Birth and the development

The life cycle of a scorpion is very interesting. There are many baby scorpions, but only limited number will live up to their maturity. It takes about 6 years to reach the maturity. The scorpions have to pass several molting stages in its life. Only limited numbers of scorpions are lucky enough to reach their maturity, as majority has to die as the results of various issues of the nature.

A female scorpion with babies on her back

There are male and female scorpions. The males can be easily identified, as they are larger than the females, and they can find each other through smell and vibrations. The animals engaged in a dance when they come across. After the mating the male should escape otherwise he will be the meal of the female. So the male used to move away before the female can get hold of him.

These creatures have a very strange method of delivering the offspring. The small ones come out of her body alive, these young ones can not live on their own, and so they live on their mother. Sometimes it lakes several weeks to leave the mothers back. The mother scorpion takes a unique position, which makes her young ones to come out of her body at the delivery stage. She waits in the position until all the babies come out, there will be 8 to 100 small ones and they are called as scorpilings. She keeps them on her back until the first molting period. Sometimes mother scorpion eats her babies.

Some people say it is one of the actions of the nature to control the members of the species. The action of the mother can control the excess members of scorpion community. After that those scorpions can have separate lives and catch their own pray.

6. Food habits of the scorpions

They are nocturnal animals, which means active at night; they hide through out the day time in cool and shady places. They usually select underground holes, decomposing logs or underside of the rocks to hide in the day time. They do not like light and they turn away from the light, because they wanted to hide them selves away from their predators. Their common enemies are birds, lizards, rats and possums.

Most of the scorpions select small anthropoids as their food, so they are predators. The larger scorpions are capable of catching bigger creatures such as rats and small lizards. They use a very creative method to catch their pray. They have large pincers to grab the victim and they are strong. The highly sensitive hairs in the pincers give the signal about the victim and the scorpion catches the pray with its pincers. Sometimes it crushes the pray or inject the victim with its venom. This venom can either kill or paralyze the victim.

- They have a unique way of eating. They use a special claw like structure, that comes out of the mouth to consume the pray. These special organs are known as chelicerae.
- The scorpion has a very primitive digestion system the digestion took place in the oral cavity.
- The scorpion puts some food into the oral cavity and the digestive enzymes are secreted in to the food and it is digested.
- They take their food in to the system as liquids.
- The remaining solids and indigestible solid matter is stored for a while and it will be thrown out by the scorpion.
- They eat a lot at one time. They have big storage and save the food, as a result of that it can spend a longer time without any kind of food there are evidence about scorpions, which have spent more than 6-12 month without another meal.
- As a result they excrete a little amount and that is consisted with solid nitrogenous compounds. Such as xanthenes and uric acid.

7. Some deadly species of scorpions

These creatures are not so popular among the people and there are about 25 deadly species of scorpions in the world. It is difficult to find a suitable vaccine or antibody for their venom, because the venom varies from species to species. There are several scorpions, which are famous for their fatal sting.

Arizona Bark scorpion

Dark colored scorpion with deadly venom, which bring fatal results for young and elderly people. The scorpion usually lies in the sand and attacks the person, who moves unsuspectingly. The young and elderly people are weak in immune system, so they are more vulnerable than the strong well built people.

Death Stalker scorpion

It is called as Israeli Yellow Scorpion by some people, but its real identity is given in the name. It is also a vastly responsible for deaths, which occurs due to scorpion sting. The scorpion may have got its name, because of its appearance and the behavior.

Emperor scorpion

The name can give the readers a vivid picture about the size of this specimen. It is larger than the other scorpions. The size of the scorpion creates a great fear in the man and it is popularly called as Imperial scorpion by people in certain parts of the world.

Fattail scorpion

This specimen is rare and it is recognized as the most dangerous killer in the scorpion family. Since the ancient times, it was known as a man killer.

Scorpion sting and the venom

All the scorpions do have venom and they use it to paralyze or kill the animals. Even the smaller ones also have the same amount of venom as their adults. Although there are more than 2000 known species of scorpions, there are only 25 species, which are fatal to the man.

The venom is not same for each and every species. It is unique to the type of the scorpion. It is consisted of large molecules called neurotoxin. They can harm the nerves of the pray. When it is injected to the body of another living being the nerve cells are attacked and the particular animal will die or get paralyzed

The symptoms of a scorpion bits

It is a very important thing to learn how to identify a scorpion sting from other bites. If we are not able to distinguish scorpion sting from other bites, we are in a very bad situation. There are only a limited number of fatal deadly scorpions. There is no need to take a lot of fear as most of the stings will be very short term and the victim will feel the pain and the warmth at the sting site.

But the deadliest bark scorpion is a thing that anyone should pay his or her attention, specially children and the elders. The victim will feel

- Pain and numbness in the sting site but there is not a swell
- The great pain in the muscles,
- The fast and uncontrollable head and eye movement

- Sweating and fast breathing
- Weakness of the body

How to treat scorpion's venom

- Clean the sting site and wash it with clean water and the soap
- Take the children to the doctor, because chidden are not so resistant like the adults.

- Sometimes the venom will be very active in certain persons, so it is better to seek medical attention.
- Take care about the symptoms and the reactions in your body.
- If it is a different place or a country, it is better to take the medical advice.

8. Scorpions and the human

- It is interesting to learn that in the traditional Chinese medicine, they have been using a wine, which is prepared of dead scorpions. It is said that it can cure many diseases.
- Scorpion is considered in the astrology as one of the zodiac sign.
- North African and South Asian countries have some cultural relationship with the scorpions. They took them as the invisible power to combat the evil. There are scorpion paintings in the Middle East countries. The scorpion has a place in Islamic religious paintings.
- The ancient Egyptians depicted one of their goddess as a scorpion. The pictures of the scorpions are found in the pyramids.
- As a whole there is not a healthy relation ship between the human and the scorpion, the man is afraid of this little predator since the ancient times. The danger of the scorpion is not a simple thing in Mexico. Annually more than 1000 people die due to deadly scorpion bites. The government tries to do its best but, as a result of hard living conditions and the environment of the country, they can not get any success.
- The scorpion is not an aggressive creature. It stings people just in case of the fear of security.

- The scorpions cannot be eliminated by using chemicals and pesticides, as they are very resistant to them. Their bodies have become resistant for those chemical components. The scorpions are sensitive to light, so we can put some outside lights in order to chase them away.
- They like to live under file of stones, wood and decomposing places, so we can get rid of those habitats in order to secure or selves from those deadly creatures.
- If there are too many and venomous species in the garden, it is better to hire an exterminator to get rid of them.

9. Myths and stories about scorpions

The scorpions have become the subject to so many myths and folk stories in the almost every country and the community of the world. There are many stories in the Asian literature.

The greedy man and the scorpion

This is one of the folk stories from Sri Lanka.Once there was a very greedy man in a village. He did not spend any money on charity or helping the community. He kept his money in a hollow of a tree in the forest and used to visit the very place to count his wealth. It was one of his daily routine.

One day a thief had seen the money and took it away. The greedy man came and learned that his money was missing. He became furious and searched and searched, but it was in vain. He did not take any food or any drink. He wanted to take the revenge and he hid behind a rock and killed the people, who used to pass the place.

The king was informed and he sent some soldiers in order to kill him. The man saw the soldiers and decided to run away but it was too late and they captured him and hanged him. Later he was born again as a scorpion, but not as a human. It was a legend in one of the Asian communities.

The great scorpion juice

A certain African tribe believes that they can get extra energy and strength by drinking scorpion juice. So they collect and consume large number of these creatures in their festivals and rituals

Amazing Animal Books Series

Learn To Draw Series

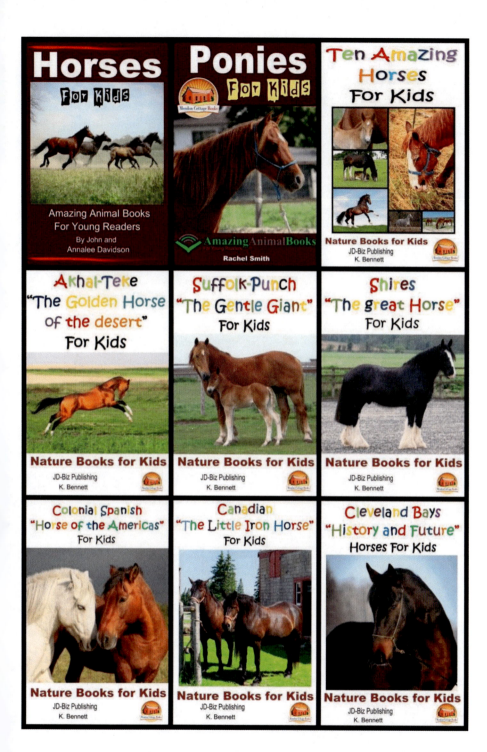

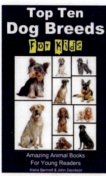

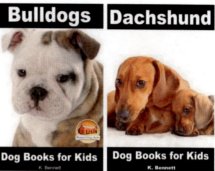

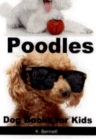

Our books are available at

1. Amazon.com
2. Barnes and Noble
3. Itunes
4. Kobo
5. Smashwords
6. Google Play Books

Download Free Books!

http://MendonCottageBooks.com

Publisher

JD-Biz Corp

P O Box 374

Mendon, Utah 84325

http://www.jd-biz.com/

Made in the USA
Columbia, SC
07 August 2022